Through Pine Shadows

THROUGH PINE SHADOWS

CAROL R. SUNDE

MoonPath Press

Poetry
ISBN 978-1-936657-86-5

Cover art: Olga Vysochynska,
Moody Pine Landscape Blue, Digital Print
ArtVisionsOlga: https://www.artfromolga.com/

Author photo: Van Adam Davis
VA Davis Photography
www.vadavisphoto.com

Book design: Tonya Namura, using
Cochin (text) and Fleur (display).

.

MoonPath Press, an imprint of Concrete Wolf Poetry Series,
is dedicated to publishing the finest poets living in the U.S.
Pacific Northwest.

MoonPath Press
c/o Concrete Wolf
PO Box 2220
Newport, OR 97365-0163

MoonPathPress@gmail.com

http://MoonPathPress.com

dedicated to my mother, father, sister, and brother
in gratitude for their forever support and love

Table of Contents

THROUGH PINE SHADOWS

Into the forest I go
to lose my mind and find my soul.
—John Muir

I

Door in the mountain
let me in.
—Jean Valentine

Life List Addition of a Tropical Species in Texas

Cyanocorax yncas

The first time ever I saw a Green Jay,
I exploded, *Well, hey-de-ho! Look at you —*
black, true blue, varied greens, yellow —
stupendously feathered creation.
And when you flew
with a changing arrangement of colors,
I exclaimed, *Wow! You do that how?*
More than fancy tail flares or wings singing wide,
more like a bedazzling jewel in flight
riding dappled light.
What a sight,
you Green Joy/Jay!
My new love!

No, not forgotten
        the Spoonbills' pink,
        an Avocet's peach breeding plumage,
        a warbler in black and white
                circling a tree trunk,
        the royal red crown of the Whooping Crane.
Yet, for now—forever, really—
it is you, Green Jay at a feeding station
filling your downy belly with grapefruit and suet
as you fill my eyes and every atom of me
then flit into the forest—
it is you who makes me want
to grow feathers, sing avian songs,
ply the sky, slip through woodlands,
line our twiggy nest
with dry grass and soft moss.

Twigs, String, Blue

Because Death hasn't yet stopped for her,
this woman continues to write and retouch memories
often released by nibbling tea-soaked madeleines.
She also applies imagination to restore
faded loves, shades of blue, family reunions
then rhythm, rhyme, or free verses them
into ever-evolving poems
using symbols, twine, twigs, rainbow-hued similes.
The efforts may enrich a piece
already including the essence
of a recent cancer scare and a cello concerto
or may begin a new composition.

When restraint like a solvent dilutes creativity,
with open-wide eyes facing fears of inadequacy,
the woman will sort through scrapbooks for lost
realities, donate blood, meditate each morning,
drive to Texas for a whooping crane encounter,
speak her mind at contentious city council meetings,
invite lonely widows over for tea.
She'll work on her life and art
until the work, never done,
is finished.

Orange and Blue

Orange flash in the yard,
then a blue-eyed cat
stops and meows to me.

Oh, orange coated cat
with blue water eyes,
do you need praise and treats?

I will give you much love,
purr admiration
for orange blue catness.

Tahoma

an homage to William Butler Yeats

I will arise and go now, and go to the mountain,
raise my yellow tent beside her White River, wander
lupine meadows, cool my toes in Shadow Lake, see firs
point to constellations, hear stars retell their stories.

I shall have some peace there as Tahoma rules the sky —
give no regard to volcano hearts waiting to explode.
Peace comes easy like the dawn, dark fears recede
in river sounds, even Jays' raucous cries seem lullabies.

I will arise and go now for always night and day I feel
Tahoma's glacier glory, hear her wind-blown songs.
Especially when I sink in sorrow, collapse in disarray,
Tahoma sends her comfort melodies directly to my soul.

Fall

hydrangea petals
fading

angle toward
ground

busy with brown
grasses

beside the fallen
fence

Time at Joshua Tree National Park

Dawn glides
a gold glow across the desert.
I drink morning water
better than the finest wine
from a glass never empty —
refreshed by heaven-sent dew.

Noon heat
gently tans a Joshua tree
stretching arms high to embrace the sun.
Among cactus flowers a road runner races —
a blurred bullet of silver feathers.
There's a pungent scent
of sand and baked fresh air.
In eon-like moments,
I forget who I am, where I am going.

Night spills
stars across the sky.
Voices hush in sleep or awe — only
nocturnal creatures rustle about
with their discreet noise. My eyes focus
up beyond Polaris and the Big Dipper
to visible/invisible galaxies.
Time scintillates
back-forward-sideways, stops.
I am present
in the infinite Now,
all sorrows set aside,
restless spirit calm.

The Partial View

Seen through a glass darkly
this world
>   where the fox lopes,
>   unaware of theologies,
>   intent on feeding the vole
>   to her little ones;
>
>   where fields of daffodils
>   shimmer gold;
>
>   where lies swarm
>   like flies over
>   the earth;
>
>   where a Mozart
>   makes music;
>
>   where waves swallow
>   fleeing refugees

my faith can falter
>   for I am no loping fox.
>   I'm like a fatherless Eve
>   exiled from Eden
>   gyrating toward Jerusalem,
>
>   a city of many mouths
>   like moths sputter-fluttering
>   words into mythical incongruities.

And yet, and yet, maybe some tomorrow —
when face to face, I shall see clearly,
know even as I am known.

In the meantime, love.

Window Reflections

The woman plopped at her desk loves
my versatility. I can let air roam
through her home, screen out flies,
provide visibility to bees
nuzzling lavender and to crows
like dark shadows in the sky
intent on mischief. She's captivated
by beach agates crowding my slide track
echoing the weather while she swills coffee,
scribbles lines like,
I'm no moon-blind horse
racing to departure.

Although I appreciate her
appropriate appreciation,
this woman denies dirt and clutter.
She's blind to the satisfaction
of neatness and my needs.
She should corral stray pencils,
polish my glass eye,
wipe my blinds white,
banish the always-shedding cat,
dust daily.

Furthermore, I shudder
at being taken for granite (pun intended):
concern means add curtains,
put up exterior shutters.

Granted I'm fastidious,
but I was meant to be unbroken transparency
in a tidy place. Surely, the woman reflects

and writes best in a clean well-lit space
where she can view me as a metaphor
for looking out and looking in.

Beach Questions Ending with a
Mary Oliver Question

Regard life as time flying faster
   than that eagle chased by crows across a clouded sky
     near a sandy seashore, watered with words
       telling tales of lost summer nights:
         could you create a more meaningful life trajectory?

Imagine you hold a cockle shell to your ear,
   listen to scrumptious sagas
     of when sailors cavorted with mermaids
       who like to tail-flip treasure maps:
         can you let yourself engage in more adventures?

Suppose you hear fur-clad ancestors articulate
   tissue and bone experiences
     into prophesies and praise
       they toss to winds or carve on stone:
         what might you learn?

Presume you eavesdrop on your deceased grandmother
   who sits by a sea reciting nursery rhymes
     while knitting red mittens
       for millions in need:
         how might you be more generous?

Visualize a cormorant slumped on cool sand
   absorb afternoon's last light as the sun retires
     below the horizon's rosy gold clouds:
       what do you plan to do
       with your one wild and precious life?

To Go to the Pond Because

so much death awaits you
like pruning shears worked diligently
                    —Adam Zagajewski

Carpe diem, the woman mutters to herself
moving down porch step carefully, recalling
Toni broke her ankle on dew-slick stairs.
She strolls by the spot where spiders fling
their filaments from rooftop to the strawberry bush,
where they weave their webs of almost invisible
silvery strands and they wait like patient buttons
until some flying bug bumps a thread.

On Surf Street where road duster grasshoppers
flare like butterflies, the woman ambles along
past a vacant lot loud with pine trees and crows.
She turns onto the path leading to the sea. Just before
the ocean dunes, there's her destination pond,
a gauge for rainfall that dips toward zero by fall.

A Great Blue Heron hunts for minnows in shore reeds.
The woman moves cautiously so she won't
frighten the bird or the Blue-eyed Darner Dragonfly
hovering close to eye her eyes before zipping off
to examine another celebrant. Nearby
willows grow large, shoulder aside rocks, grouse
about nothing. Plump blackberries look ready
to become wine. The woman imagines Franciscans
anointing the heron and herself with blessings
poured from a warm yellow tea pot.

Alone but not alone, settling herself in dune grass,
the woman lets go of all worries, deeply inhales
a gospel written in pond ripples, in sun-dipped lines.

II

*I carry inside myself my earlier
faces, as a tree contains rings.*
—Tomas Transtromer

I'd Like to Lie Like the Sea Lies

If I imply Mother is a mermaid,
Father an angelfish, Sister a gull,
Brother a Finnish sailor,
and I a landlocked orca—
please accept my little fibs.

Maybe I'll mention how I ride
a sea horse where ocean waves
throw stones against the shore;
how I beg Neptune to reform me
into a vessel worthy of any journey.

Or, I'll claim I swim wearing golden scales
and plumage stolen from a dragon's tail.
Watch me sink through kelp with dolphins,
drink oceans till I flow like jellies—
my myths preserved in brine.

But know beneath deceptive surfaces,
say forty fathoms deep, alter egos
using sea pens and octopus ink
write my true history:
my calms and squalls alike.

Absence

Way too soon, Death stole Dad
leaving his wife, two daughters
too young to remember him,
and an unborn son.

Black and white, blurred by time — Easter
by the basket of candy eggs my sister clutches —
my favorite picture of Dad:
beside our farmhouse, a moonfaced Norwegian
dressed for church beams his pleasure
posing with his daughters. He cradles
me to his chest, Ella leans against his leg.

We would visit him annually at West Prairie,
plant geraniums beside his tombstone,
then let that good man stay buried.

As a child, I felt special:
our Daddy was dead.
As a teen, I sensed the empty space.

If he'd lived, we kids
would have grown up on the farm
instead of in town,
named our dog Frigg
instead of Princess.
Mom might have smiled more.
Would I recognize the me I'd be?

A Story Told About the Father
We Never Knew

Afternoon torrents of freezing wind and snow lashed
the farm, all creatures and creation. The house crackled,
groaned like a ship caught in a white-whipped sea
and that sea became a nebulous monster devouring
distance and escape. An old oak tree snapped, bare
branches slapped hard ground, broke. Mable, the dog,
and Loki, the cat, usually enemies, cuddled together
under a bed. Collecting you kids on the couch, your
Mom held each one close while your Dad heavy with
fat jacket, coveralls, gloves, cap, boots, life-line fastened
himself to a porch pole, then forced his way through
the storm to assure each chicken roosted safe in their
coop and to tightly secure the barn door so the cows and
horses huddled inside would have needed warmth and
protection. On his way, spotting three snow-n-ice blind
pheasants plastered against a fencepost, he gathered the
half-frozen birds in his arms and carefully settled them
onto the straw of an empty horse stall before resuming
his planned chores. When a serene world glistened in
morning sun, when everyone could see again, your
father, a good shepherd, herded the pheasant flock into
the new day.

Full of compassion,
he'd never choose to leave you:
he loved you too much.

A Detail from My Will

I've secured my pet
sorrow in a bird cage.

Let it fly free
after I die but

beware its rage roiling
like a sabotaged tomorrow.

Remembering 1950 Thanksgiving Days

Over the meadow and through the woods
to Grandmother's house we go.

Iowa November brings snowflakes and a chilling wind
that pulls off the few oak leaves still clinging to branches,
tosses brown-gold-red leaves like notes every which way,
lets them sail groundward to be read or not.
Oak skeletons stretch silhouetted against slate skies,
their bony limbs scratch low clouds.

Every Thanksgiving Day,
Great-Aunt-Annie-Great-Uncle-Eddie's small boxy home
sitting unobtrusively on the edge of small town Leland
becomes boisterous—packed with Grandma, Grandpa,
aunts, uncles, cousins, sisters, brothers, tables, chairs,
laughter, talking, and noise mingling with aromas
of potluck offerings loaded on every inch of counter space.
Flicka, the house cat, crawls under a coat-covered bed
far from what she perceives to be the *madding crowd*,
her tail over her eyes and ears to wait out this annual
invasion.

Before we pray
     Thank you, God for the world so sweet,
     Thank you for the food we eat,
     Thank you for the birds that sing,
     Thank you, God, for all good things

before we feast on
     Turkey and ham, Apple and sage stuffing, Mashed
     potatoes and gravy, Sweet potatoes, Coleslaw, Red
     cabbage salad, Creamed corn, Green bean
     casserole, Rolls, Lefse, Biscuits, Pumpkin pie,

Pecan pie, Fudge, Krumkake, Milk, Kool-aide,
Cider, and Coffee

we all take a turn sharing something we are thankful
for—Uncle Andrew always begins.

Uncle Andrew: *I'm thankful "The heavens declare
the glory of God and the firmament
showeth his handiwork." Psalm 19:1.*
Grandma: *I'm thankful for family being together.*
Aunt Lucille: *For good health.*
Cousin Jerry: *Pie.*
Uncle Grover: *The fine corn crop this year.*
Cousin Gwen: *My new blue warm winter coat.*
Mom: *For all this tasty food everyone brought.*
Sister Ella: *I'm thankful for wonderful Mom.*
Uncle Henry: *That my truck still runs.*
Auntie Ethel: *For a robin, pigeon, peony, lilac world.*
Brother Carl: *Our set of encyclopedias.*
Great Aunt Annie: *The taste of strong coffee
every morning.*
Cousin Charles: *My new job at The Best Grocery Store.*
Cousin Stanley: *I'm thankful I passed my algebra test.*
Cousin Jane: *Indoor plumbing.*
Cousin John: *Our winning Lake Mills football team.*
Cousin Judy: *Pretty sunrises and sunsets.*
Grandpa: *For words like green, rain, sun, punctilious.*
Cousin Loren: *I'm thankful for my pet pig, Jolly.*
Me: *My flute even though I can't play it very good.*
Cousin Leo: *The turkey sacrificed for this meal.*
Great Uncle Eddie: *I'm thankful for those who serve our
country—soldiers, nurses, teachers, preachers, firefighters.*
Cousin Miriam: *That Christmas is just around the corner.*
Aunt Gen: *For the West Prairie Lutheran Church people.*
Aunt Irene: *All the joys of being alive.*

After our banquet
>some sit and gossip about the neighbors;
>some play rook, checkers, or monopoly;
>some walk down town to gawk
>at shop window mannequins
>dressed for the holidays;
>some gather around the piano to sing
>when Mom plays and Grandpa fiddles
>*You Are My Sunshine, Red Wing, O Happy Day;*
>some help clean up;
>some just sit.

When   *Now the day is over*
>*Night is drawing nigh*
>*Shadows of the evening*
>*Steal across the sky*

we say goodbye with polite Norwegian hugs; head home
thankful for this Thanksgiving Day. Hearing the quiet,
Flicka sneaks out from under the now coatless bed,
reclaims her domain. She enjoys turkey scraps for supper
then climbs onto Great Uncle Eddie's ample lap for petting
time as November snow calmly falls covering ground,
houses, trees, town.

Misfit

When champagne is needed, I suggest cod liver oil.
In a string quartet, I am a gate-crashing tuba.

When others smile, I often smirk.
In a bowlful of sweet plums, I am a fiery radish.

Among nasturtiums, I am a thistle.
Yet some few do appreciate me——

certain goats and sheep in spring,
songbirds when I have gone to seed—

Eating Kith and Kin

I. Auntie Ethel, city-dweller, the 1930s

Pigeons swarm the stoop
where Ethel hunches crumbling stale bread
to bits that litter her tattered skirt.
Audible despite neighborhood racket,
she purrs soft as cat fur:
> *Well, come into my range*
> *then into my range. Sweet Pigeon,*
> *meet your destiny with grace.*
> *I mind the deed but*
> *we need protein.*
> *We'll honor your passing*
> *with Bach as you bake.*

Ever agile, Ethel grabs a gray bird
who landed too close and soon
it's browning meat
to "Jesu, Joy of Man's Desiring."

II. Grandpa, farmer, the 1940s

Our tribe, hushed for the ritual,
gathers out of sight and sound
of the kitchen where aunties cluck
over coffee, prepare potatoes, rolls, green beans —
and away from the henhouse
where abductions disturb that home's sanctity.
Sam, Lois, and Mary upended by their scrawny legs,
bagged, and carried off.

From a burlap sack, Grandpa pulls
the large leghorn, cockscomb blindfolding one eye.

29

Grasping its head, he raises his arm as if in blessing,
then twirls the chicken's body until head separates from neck.

Sometimes headless birds struggle from the ground
to flip-flop dance in this transmutation spectacle.

Canticle for Auntie Ethel

Auntie Ethel hands out red-n-white peppermints,
reads from her Bible heavy with bookmarks

in a mother's voice crooning a lullaby,
The lord is my shepherd . . .

Grandma's sofa holds her, brother,
sister, cousins, me, the dog. Our bodies

lie down in green pastures,
while Spud's tail beats a steady thump-thump

beside the still waters. Uncle Andrew joins us
silently reciting,

I will fear no evil.
My head rests on Auntie's shoulder,

thou art with me — her church dress
smooth as milk and her faint lilac scent

comfort like a goodnight kiss.
My cup runneth over.

She finishes, *in the house of the Lord forever,*
and motions for us to follow tip-toe to the barn.

We see Red Hen's brown eggs
miraculously transformed to yellow chicks.

Over the Moon

Those cows are outstanding
in their field. The pun always
tickles my big sister, Ella.

She shares it with Lulu and Blue
mouthing their cud — the pasture
fragrant with manure and morning.

Hearing their receptive moos,
Ella grins, scrambles over the fence,
skips around the cows chanting,

Hey, diddle, diddle!
The cat and the fiddle,
The cow jumped over the moon.

From Gram's porch, I scowl
drenched in gloom, wishing to be
my smart pretty sister.

Ella yells, *Come on, swing time.*
We scamper to the oak tree hung
with straw-stuffed gunny sacks,

run, jump, straddle the bags, and sail
up and down the sky together
under the sun and over the moon.

One Long Held Breath at the State Music Contest

Gold light sieved through window screens
coloring the performance platform warm.
Judges smiled, Mom threw a thumbs-up,
my piano accompanist nodded, *Go.*
My agile fingers followed Mozart's notes
until they quit.

Silence, loneliness, then
dirty shame. No one forgets
half their solo. No one.

     Only hours ago,
the van chugged to Iowa City
filled with students eager for honor.
Ella hugged her cello and pretended to sleep.
Warren kept swearing, *No flats.*
Toni self-hypnotized sailing by the cornfields.
Friends since first grade, Shirley and I practiced
our performance pieces in air.

     Only minutes ago,
my playing *Andante in F* surely
could be determined noteworthy.
How could my brain and fingers fail,
my magic flute shape shift to ordinary stick?
Why should failure hurt worse
than stepping barefoot on a barn nail
like I did last summer?

The noise of soundless howling.
A long held breath to stop the world.

Only after forever,
I heard Shirley inside my head,
Oh, get over yourself and Mom promising,
Mozart will forgive you.
When my accompanist hissed,
Breathe — breathe — begin again,
I think I did — and maybe even finished
to hands clapping.

Horses

From nearby
dry hilltops
my friend and I
hear a herd
of horses
horsing around —
snorts, nickering,
neighs, whinnies —
hoarse, earthy,
nothing coarse.

Some broad
perched aboard
a mare's
broad bare
back, scans
for bear.
Her *Giddy-up*

starts horses
coursing, rumbling
toward plains
plainly visible
down through
downed trees
into sweet
green pastures.

Moved, we
don't move.
Charlie lists
three reasons
why Poe
could copy

the poet
Li Po
then he
kisses me.

Although I'm No Moses

Dear Lord, return me
to my child-self
whose ears burned as You
talked to and about me.

Wandering dense woods,
now I don't hear Your words
even rustle in wind rushing
through dried brush

despite listening hard
for the lightest sound
flickering in
tangled thickets.

Help me climb a mountain,
discover a shrub lit bright
with You speaking through flames
crackling with love's reassurance.

Touch me, torch me with Your voice,
ignite insight in my bones,
scorch doubt, cremate confusion,
consume emptiness.

III

Was it all a dream —
I mean those by-gone days —
were they what they seemed?
All night I lie awake
listening to autumn rain.
—Taigu Ryokan

Yesterday's Superstition

Women circle the frame,
like carefree children
released from chores,

lay out flour sack patches
to piece an heirloom
together, laughing

as work-calloused hands
sew joys and heartaches into quilts.
From remnants, roses

grow from one sack's red,
stems and leaves from a green.
Lest God be jealous

of such pleasure,
one flaw is included in their art—
perhaps a misplaced tendril.

With my quilts I fear
defects more than God's annoyance—
and seek a faultless cover.

Remember that old saying,
*You will marry next
if a quilt-tossed cat lands near you?*

No doubt, an angry cat would have
snubbed me and, like my quest
for perfection, doom romance.

Grandma once asked, *Say life's
a quilt, will yours be one
embroidered with rue?*

How to Comfort a Cold

Let it rest on your sofa
slurping lots of hot chocolate.
Even if provoked,
do not complain or frown.

Fire up the furnace.
Provide your best eiderdown quilt.
Remove all albatrosses.
Suggest a lilac-scented sauna.

Wear interesting pajamas.
Dance the coughing-slipper-shuffle.
Tell the funny story
about how you broke your tibia.

Don't defiantly recite from "Invictus,"
I am the master of my fate.
Understand a cold
has its own reasons for being.

Refuge

Horizon and sky close in
as marine mist stealthily
obscures ocean, land, space —

no wide, wondrous worlds
in this cloudy enclosure.
Yet pleasures abound

without the expanse,
the demands
to see too much.

Sand slippers my feet,
muffled foghorns play the blues,
wind is my masseuse.

In this place circled
with soft nimbus walls,
war, disease, evil

dampen, diminish
in sea fragrance, solitude,
salt taste on the tongue.

Return

We sang, *Holy, holy, holy, Lord God Almighty,* Sundays
        after Mom lead us dressed in our Thrift Shop best
into the cross-laden, candle-scented Lutheran Church,
        bigger and better than the Catholic one
and a plain Baptist structure near the railroad tracks.

The weekly ritual — scripture, thunderous
        organ accompaniment to hymns, prayers,
long sermon, communion, and sometimes a baptism
        all shared with neighbor, friend, stranger —
reassuring as spring's first trillium.

Older now, belief-eroded, far gone
        from childhood security, often feeling godforsaken,
I wear life scars like survival tattoos, disrupt
        my desired Buber's I-Thou balanced scale by
heavier weighting the I, and don't faithfully attend church.

Yet when I crave *Jesus-loves-me* nourishment
        I don't believe in but do; hunger to sit at supper
with doubting Thomas, patient Mary, righteous Martin;
        need to consider the cross and sing praise;
I slip into a Lutheran service a welcome prodigal daughter.

Late Afternoon at Ridgefield Wildlife Refuge

A clean slate of sky waits to be chalked up
with migrations. Light intensifies
yellows and rusts of wetland brush.
And the light becomes a presence
that weaves among reeds, spangles
on streams, filters gold around us,
the sandhill crane seekers.

Behind a blind, we're a motley group
gathered on a small grassy patch
expanded by slanted light and good will.
We're pilgrims ready to be amazed
by huge gray birds descending from on high
to eat and rest.

While cranes like honking beads
string across a far corner of sky,
Jacob downs coffee, offers to share.
Lily and her little brother dominate
a scope, celebrate each mallard, and ensure
everyone has a close-up turn. Barbara retreats
to light a cigarette. The newlyweds, Jake and May,
make room on a log for elderly Al.

When the sun hunkers near the horizon,
a cloud of sandhill cranes flaps
through peach light. The birds call out,
drop before us to embrace marshy ground —
otherworldly creatures careening
toward earth and us after a long flight.

I feel light.
I'm a light wind flowing home.

Grounded with friends and birds, I want
to kneel and shout, *Thank you. Thank you
for open skies, open waters, fields full of food,
journeys that end in safe havens.*

Instead I smile, speechless,
one with the congregation.
Twilight wraps us in bliss.
In remote woods, coyotes yip and yodel.
The sandhill cranes bugle, ready
for a good night.

Slow Time

Snow enfolds the valley
with a softness softer
than the lightest fleece.

Through long nights
and short days,
retreating winds

hush each blizzard;
returning winds
hobble our hours.

Cold hibernates us,
a lucky couple.
Under snow-knowing time

we learn tranquility
lying sleepy close
while winter light

drifts in the white valley,
into our white room,
onto our bed, our bodies.

Eye Examination

after Ho Xuan Huong, translated by John Balaban

My pupils dilate.

He soothes, *Breathe,*

look into my eyes.

Open wide.

He leans toward me

instrument ready,

wanting to

explore me closely —

he's so careful, I could cry.

Freudian Pink Slip

I thought myself attentive
    to the rushing Elk River and the road

        as I drove to our secret tryst,

despite reveling in my memory
    of your voice as you laughed

        at the direction aptness of *Exit*,

pursued by a bear, before I knew
    what you meant. Perhaps unconscious

        guilt distracted me from seeing

as it leapt into reality —
    a deer soaring over the hood

        aimed right at me —

your wife-the-wide-eyed-doe
    I braked and swerved to miss.

        There was no crash or red splashing

the white Corolla, just me veering
    off the road —

        missing your wife

and you. I stared unseeing
    at trees for hours,

        slow to understand.

Unacceptable Departure

Daisies have
                no   disk,

trains   no
tracks,
                                crows
                no   caw,

canyons   no
depth,

books   no
                                words.

The sun   is   ice.

Without who I thought you were,
my forever friend and lover,
I only manage living
by lying you'll return.

To-do List

Coffee and toast

Read today's news written yesterday

Do not hover near the stairwell
listening for absent footsteps

Notice against the almond tree
like an unplanned memorial
the old ladder he forgot
to put away

Recall that Baja trip
       how on the beach
       that star-radiant night
       feeling so limp and light
       we levitated

Love Story

Over four summer-infused years,
my darling declared forever love,
cherished me like a gemstone
of stupendous value

and then he left

not like a hungry deer
who steps delicately away
from a rose bush
doused in repellant stench;

not like a cardinal
brightening a naked maple
briefly, then fleeing
to trees dressed in green;

more like a fountain
of bubbling water
slowly frozen
over a long winter.

So this is my story:

     Love came calling,
opened the gate,
     rocked awhile
on my porch swing,
     drank a beer,
belched, and left,
     leaving the empty can
to be recycled.

Fairy Tale Redux

Not such a nobleman after all,
you rode away on a lame horse,

corroded armor clanking,
to hunt new prey.

You took our falcon,
spurned our dog.

Hey-de-ho Ole Prince,
gone these many years

perhaps you're dead
or wish you were

if appropriately tortured
by regrets. And me?

For far too long, you were as essential
as water in a desert. I wailed,

*Come back, Liebchen, and drag
remorse like stones in your wolf belly.*

Gradually, I let reality seep in
and learned to rescue myself.

From miles of blue thread
I wove a robe of forgiveness,

let my hair grow strong
and useful like Rapunzel's,

took spin-straw-into-gold lessons,
tossed dated Cinderella slippers,

dropped my own pebbles
to mark the way home.

A Regressive Step

As Shirley and I, "not that old" hikers, sidle
past a boulder on Hurricane Hill,
it happens again. This time
a puffing teenager gasps,
You two are an inspiration.

Shirley's rehearsed retort oozes syrup,
*Why, kiddo, how sweet but we're lost. You seen
the casino that serves the early bird special?*
I mutter, *What to do, what to do?*
Rocking chair broke. Knitting snarled.

The girl's flushed
face pales.
Scrambling away,
she calls back,
Sorry.

No longer do I see
the undulating hills' green variations
or taste the breeze fresh from a cloudless sky.
Ashamed, I hear myself in a red-tailed hawk shriek,
feel my talons puncturing a hapless prey.

Out from Under

This woman learns living in Tacoma
sometimes means limited visibility and why
Mount Rainier-Tahoma-The Mountain
is worshipped:
O Landscape-commander,
O Weather-maker.

When Tahoma relaxes in sunshine
wearing her green skirt and snow top,
the woman hums *Rock-a My Soul.*
When clouds cling like chubby blindfolds
smothering poor Tahoma,
in sympathy she barely breathes.

When too many books, nicknacks, and bills
pile up like punishing Puritan stones on her chest,
the woman deserts Tacoma for The Mountain,
vowing upon return to unclutter, toss the trivial,
live as minimalist—
more saintly.

After wine by a cozy fire, viewing
the comfortably distant stars' infernos,
the woman curls deep into her sleeping bag,
dreams riffraff becomes Fay Fuller resplendent
in a blanketed dress designed for climbing.
She and Fay summit Mount Rainier.

When the woman wakes to conifers lolling
in sunshine and her camp bear-clean,
she senses an ineffable presence
inviting her to cast off what doesn't matter.
She acknowledges she's like Tahoma:
she can make her own weather.

High Desert Wetlands

You can step into a Malheur night
in this oasis for the avocet,
antelope, and weary ones;

grab fistfuls of stars
without interference
from any city's bully lights.

Perhaps you'll be reminded of the Sabbath —
        Muir would have seen all the temple we need
        in this boundless marsh and sagebrush serenity,
        the view all the way to heaven —
and you put aside grievances to praise.

The Shell

During a misty beach walk,
I pick up a clam half-shell still wave wet,
its shallow bowl interior a milky way
circled by washed-out blue
with navy dashes marking the edges.
Growth rings rounding its exterior
evoke "The Chambered Nautilus" lines:

> *Build thee more stately mansions, O my soul,*
> *Till thou at length art free.*

I think of the common murre I'd seen earlier
laid out by a high tide on the shore
in elegant death:
white breast bone exposed,
wings still flying,
eyes closed with sparkling sand.

As usual, I return the shell to its resting place
but I stow its image inside myself
so I can remember, travel back in time,
be by the ocean to praise and mourn
clam and bird,
hear Holmes' words like a muted foghorn.

Hike with Dead Cat

My adored Whitman,
my deceased cat grown vague with time, leaps
onto my sleeping bag. Only half-awake I
believe he's real — at least, a heavy spirit.

When morning begins as an overture
to a symphony new to me, I break camp singing
with Whitman a muffled accompaniment
to follow a trail reviewed as spectacular.

From pine tops, red squirrels, those chittering
piccolos, alert the world of our approach
and grouse skedaddle, rustling
like brushed drums, deep into salal.

Near a lake reflecting the Teton Mountains,
a love ballet——two sandhill cranes
twirl, flap, and bow to music
only they can hear.

My feet begin drumming
on the trail, my spine tingles
like a tapped xylophone,
harmony hums through my body

and I recognize — enfolding
mountains, lake, cranes, and me —
Whitman's robust,
resurrected melody.

Deposed

In spring, farmhands secured her to a post
wearing corncob shoes, faded purple dress,
foil crown on her pillow head, looking lost
not royal, even at her youthful best.

Her eerie stance could command all stray cows,
trespassing chickens, deer, and crows away.
Through heat and rain, she'd act stern queen yet bow
with breezes, summon clouds to come and play.

Now wind-battered, she tilts awry in snow;
her body leaks hay over the white page.
Enemies fled—cold leaves nothing growing
to guard. Light ebbs but still reveals her age.

Every reign must end. Let her tumble down
and rest. Her season is done. Take her crown.

Reckoning in Three Acts with Butterflies

1. What Was

When I was young and pretty,
stardust in my eyes,
I joined a traveling theater troupe,
fell in lust/love with a leading man
and this Mr. Tall-Dark-and-Handsome asked
me to marry him. *Yes*, I cried, *Yes.*
Let's marry, be merry forever together.
At our outdoor wedding,
a Silvery Blue butterfly settled
on my hair for a long moment.

When this Mr. Right turned Mr. Wrong
(money feuds, the affair, lies),
we tried to find our love again
through counseling and forgiveness
but couldn't. We put away each other
hoping for someone, something better.

2. What Is

With many years trailing behind me,
among the things I've learned:
I may want a man but do not need one.

This morning, from a dream of clouds
erasing my existence, I notice
Gram's quilt on the wall releasing
its butterflies that never fly,
only open and close their wings
in gentle gestures just before
the alarm clock announces,
Wake up! It's time! Wake up!

From nowhere a memory jumps into consciousness:
that man in Starbucks asking who I was reading.
He sat nearby jabbering on and on about Patterson,
his favorite author, as I planned a polite escape.
The next day, he's at my door, handing me a handful
of his hand–picked daisies.
(How did he find my home?)
I hesitated, took the flowers,
forced a smile, said *Thank you*, and closed the door.

3. What Will Be

Disintegration
looms not far away
when eyes, hands, brain, heart . . .
well-worn, will wear out
but then, no doubt,

Angelwing butterflies
will beckon me home
because it's time to lie down
    and sleep,
        and sleep,
           and sleep.
I hope to sleep pretty
dead satisfied.

IV

The darkness quiets,
if we watch it together.
—Charlotte Pence

Past Seventy I Talk to Birds

Today cormorants like dull ornaments
pose on Chehalis River pilings.

No sun shines to dry
their wings stretched and hung

like sodden little mourning cloaks,
dripping into the harbor.

*Sometimes I wish I were already
flown beyond familiar shores,*

*but tell me, O you Cormorants,
wouldn't I regret all the lost fish?*

Gulls complain.
Otherwise, silence.

Wondering in a Utah Canyon

Before this autumn, why haven't I heard
the aspens in their yellow leaf quiver
sing answers to re-occurring questions?
      Do I belong?
      Don't most hearts harbor loving kindness?
      Does a good god exist?

Once I listened to a choir of crows vocalize
and their ascending caws scored a note
across a nearby blank monolith:
      In this concert, everything plays
      its part as conducted, even as a mountain lion
      leaps on a doe's back, ending one solo.

Camping by this canyon's Green River
burbling in its pebbled bed,
I wonder,
      Why not be composed: value questions,
      music, dissonance; savor slices
      of famous sweet Utah watermelon?

Billy Frank Jr. Nisqually National Wildlife Refuge

Hoping to find "peace like a river,"
quiet myself among alders, owls, and blue-eyed grass,
I ease my car from thick afternoon traffic
into the protected estuary.

By the brackish visitor pond,
a little girl jabbing her finger this way and that,
whispers, *There! They're everywhere. Look! Look!*
My frown erased, my eyes softening, I see
by a log near the cattails, peering from lily pads,
blended in as still as stones—red-legged frogs.
Love them frogs, I murmur, *thanks for sharing.*

Heading toward the Twin Barns, I stroll
through a shower of cottonwood catkins
as a loud low *moo* rises from the bog.
Noticing my what-is-that face,
a boy setting up a bird scope explains, *Bullfrog.*
We watch a red-winged blackbird
ride a reed down to the water to drink.
Exchanging smiles, we sigh, *Yes, yes, oh yes.*

In an avian show by the barns, with breakneck speed,
swallows zoom and zig-zag, scoop insects from the air,
swoop to mud nests tucked under eaves—to feed babies
before performing a sleek-feathered rush skyward again.
Ever so slowly twilight slides this day aside
preparing for the moon's arrival.
A ladybug lands on my shoulder bringing
a greeting, a recognition, a benediction.

Beyond Nisqually

I scuttle a shady path
at the Refuge, more than a little wild,
scuffle leaves
      where crisp breezes hula rose hips
      and snowberries bead bushes.
I imagine plover, goose, godwit
engines fueling
migrations south
      as maples unclasp
      autumn fashions, strip
      leaf after leaf
      to slither and glide
      down trunk and limbs,
      exposing intimations
      of what the future holds.

No birds chatter about dire portents though,
even as my inner ear corrupts
balance, the way of the upright
I thought I'd mastered;
      occasionally I lurch sideways
      like a feeble coot
      hell-bent on staying vertical
      until it's time to rise heavenward.

Salt Loses Savor

My years stacked high, I have a hard time
talking with the living and the dead.

I don't understand my long gone Auntie Ethel's sputter,
I may not be fast, but I am slow.

        ~

When I mention to a neighbor that building
big bonfires in a south blowing wind means
I get his smoke at my house, he snaps, *So.*
I hustle home like a hawk-threatened chicken.
Recalling the adage about a carrot
working better than a stick with donkeys,
I stare out a window looking for what to say
in an effective carrot way.

        ~

Cousin Warren often chuckles as if he's forgotten
he fell from the air in flames over Viet Nam
to a death no medal could justify.
I always remind Warren I prayed for peace
and still pray, *Dear God, help us find peace,*
even as my brain shrinks and my tongue stutters
after elusive words and I feel my once plummy skin
dry to a prune no one touches.

        ~

Some nights, just before I drift asleep,
Charlie, my second and best love, who disappeared
in a fog of disappointments, reappears bragging,
We were good together for awhile —lusty alive.
 I reply, *Maybe.*

        ~

Last week, dear old Shirley forgot my birthday.
Today as we eat old cake, she chirps, *Oops!*
to my sigh, *I wanted celebratory fireworks.*

For the umpteenth time Shirley asks,
Whatever happened to Toni?

Auntie Ethel's ever present spirit patiently repeats,
Surely goodness and mercy shall follow.

After the Call

How shall the heart be reconciled
to its feast of losses?
　　　　　　—Stanley Kunitz

A burnt coffee taste in my mouth,
I dash the half mile to the ocean.
Dune grass slaps my legs,
clouds bury the sky.

Waves repeat, *Your mother is gone.*
Sea winds moan litanies
as I mechanically scan the tide's offerings.

From sand dollars, kelp, and feathers
I rescue a beach agate —
hold in my cold hard hand
a miniature mountain.

The amber stone with rust-colored veins
gleams from every angle —
each crystal slope, each etched crevice.

A keeper,
Mom would have said.
See how it contains
yet lets brightness through.

Despite a bitter Iowa winter,
why didn't I go back
for her last birthday?

She was/is my rock, my beach agate
inviting sunlight to enter,
dwell within, then shine,
a beacon for sweet and sour times.

Mystics Affirm Union with God Is Blue Light

As the sun crawls up
a rooster's waking crow,
sky curving over my head
like a blue bonnet
is what I need.
        Since Mom
followed Dad to sleep
in supposed peace,
I've played
the shipwrecked,
orphaned kitten
dashed ashore
like one soggy
mitten unraveled
by wool-gathering fools.
        Blue,
I'm tired of being wired
to self-imposed wrongs
so long. Stop
my wallowing
and tune my whine
to intoning
some celestial jazz.
        Blue,
be my ceiling,
my floor, my stairway;
lend me an agate
talisman to tuck
into an empty pocket;
send rockets
to skywrite clues
to what's true

and what's egotism
or useless myth.
        Splatter indigo
everywhere it matters.
Free me
from embracing
new bruises.

My Sister and I Visit Our Parents at West Prairie

Like a heaving green sea,
corn and bean fields roll
over low Iowa hills to the horizon.
Centered in green waves,
the white Lutheran church floats
at anchor with a graveyard in tow
holding our parents.

"Not my will, but thine be done"
carved on Dad's tombstone seems
more resignation than comfort
considering Mom's lament,
*He died too young. Before
his children could know him.*

After decades, Mom and Dad
lie next to each other.
We slouch, old orphans before them,
offer roses and plant geraniums.

Sis and I meander among the dead
from the late eighteen hundreds to a month ago.
We pull mean weeds defacing monuments
with weather-erased names.

Some markers crumble,
several lean ready to rest,
the recent stand strong —
a gracious green sea waits.

Aging with Blind Variations

I'm losing my vision,
another derision.

Even with corrective lens,
clarity's a farce —

my version of the good-
to-come also distorted.

But when I close my eyes,
sleep, I find it paradise

to wake and see again
all the beauty I can —

       moon, peace, bogs, trees, roads, love,
       dogs, loons, toads, kindness, clover —

conscious of what I'll miss
if I live in willful blindness.

Dear Ones,

(Who, if I cried out,
would heed me —
if you listened?

And still I call out.)

Whoever you are, go out into the morning
when the birds sing
to walk inside yourself.

Just be.
Diving ducks will dabble in shallow water.
Kestrels hover and drop straight down
slipping through the molecules.
Reflected in the eye of the owl
is a great rose window of a cathedral.
Loons, known for their haunting wail,
wail songs that tumble through the air.

Try asking:
What wonders are these?
Why is there so much love in them —
hope, the thing with feathers?

In your quest to escape from a sadness shell,
bring your outer and inner lives into harmony.
Be patient with everything unresolved in your heart.
With the grace of air-curved feathers and lifted wing,
launch into another world.

Dear Ones,
it's never too late for rhapsody.

Once and Then and Then

My love and I once stood toe to toe
with a Galapagos blue-footed booby.
Kathmandu pigeons once woke us
to living Himalayan legends. Once
we feasted on scrumptious strawberries
awash in foamy cream and argued
about who should clean the garage.
Everything, even quarrels, once
flavored with rapture.

After our split, hiking Six Glaciers trail alone
meant six changing views of Lake Louise
and who I might be
traveling solo.

Time went on and I went on
reconstructing myself one small action at a time.
I let break-up bitterness and loneliness dissolve
in countless cups of coffee shared with friends
as we celebrated
       vermilion sunsets over pine-perfumed forests
       and counseling a D student toward a B
       and a Debussy recital that sent us
       warbling all the way home
as well as bemoaned
       cancer killing Toni's mother
       and wildfires blasting trees to ashes
       and dead children, collateral damage
       in a drive-by shootings.

Now looking back
at my elegant and flawed life
tangled in knots of glory and decay —
        robin azure eggs   never hatched,
        cathedral walls   wounded by bullets,
        love found   love lost —
whatever the luck, whatever the choices,
tarnation and hallelujah, here I am. Here I am.

Goodnight with Flights of Angels Singing

Across boundary waters,
      a loon calls,
and, as I unroll
      my sleeping bag,
annoyances fade:
      that sputtering campfire,
a ripped pack strap,
      your grumbles about
our endless hike.

A loon call is the last sound
      I hear — haunting
lonely loveliness — before
      I sleep.

Someday when we finish
      our final *love you-*
love you, too,
      I'd like to die
hearing a loon call.

Moonlit Walk

Day is ending
cool with snow
drifting down
like crystal
flower petals.
As if wanting
to show the way,
three song sparrows
bounce along a path
in front of me.
My purple sequined boots
inspire prancing,
pirouettes, even polka hops,
but I stroll slowly,
watch and await
the appearance of words
I can use to truly
express gratitude
to everyone and everything
that warms me.
I look up, down,
and all around.
In moonbeams,
I see suspended
a maple's last leaves
wrinkle, curl, and shape
into letters spelling out
in every imaginable language,
thank you, merci, gracias . . .

A Place to Linger

By the side of a river
I will lay down
my sorrows
and drowse.

In a dandelion haze,
enchanting winds
mumble, embrace
and caress me

with the softness
of a hummingbird's
easy breathing
breast feathers.

When I rouse,
I lift my eyes
skyward and see
blue quiet, mellow sun.

Walking home
through pine shadows,
the path is paved
with cushiony moss.

Notes

"Billy Frank Jr. Nisqually Wildlife Refuge."
The phrase "peace like a river" is from the Horatio
Spafford hymn "It is Well with My Soul" also known as
"When Peace Like a River."

"Dear Ones,"
This poem is a written in a modified cento form which
means it is constructed using only the words of others
but it does have some minor adjustments for coherence.
Credits are listed below. All the referenced poems by
Rainer Maria Rilke are in *Rilke: New Poems* translated by
Joseph Cadora. The phrases and sentences by other
poets can be found in *The Poets' Guide to Birds*, edited by
Judith Kitchen and Ted Kooser.

Line Credits:

2-3   Rilke, quoted by Robert Hass, "Foreword" to
      Rilke: New Poems, p. xvii

4   Rilke, "Buddha"

5   Rilke, "The Temptation"

6   Rilke, quoted by Hass, "Foreword" in *Rilke: New
      Poems*, p. xvi

7   Haskins, Lola, "When the Birds Sing"

8   Rilke, *Letter to a Young Poet*, p. 54

10   Sibley, David, *Field Guide to Birds of Western North
      America*, p. 73

11   Sibley, *Field Guide . . .* p. 115

12   Franklin, Ken, quoted by Thor Hanson, in *Feathers*,
      p.135

13-14 Cadora, Joseph, "Introduction" in *Rilke: New Poems*,
      makes reference to a Rilke poem, p. xxix

15 Sibley, *Field Guide* . . . p. 26

16 Brehm, John, "Song Bird"

18 Black, Ralph, "Birds of Prayer"

19 Rilke, "Beruinage"

20 Dickenson, Emily quoted in *Feathers*, p. 6

21 Short, Lester, *The Lives of Birds*, p. 3

22 Rilke, *Letters to a Young Poet*, translated by Stephen Mitchell, p.100

23 Rilke, *Letters to a Young Poet*, translated by Mitchell, p. 34

24 Wetmore, Alexander and other ornithologists, *Song and Garden Birds of North America*, p.13

25 Moore, Jim, "Near Herons"

27 Funkhouser, Erica, "Owl Pellet"

"Eye Examination"
Ho Xuan Houng's poems often include sexual innuendos.

"Fairy Tale Redux"
References are made to several stories in *Grimms' Fairy Tales* .

"Freudian Pink Slip"
The phrase "Exit, pursued by a bear" is a stage direction from Shakespeare's *The Winter's Tale.*

"High Desert Wetlands"
Malheur National Wildlife Refuge is in southeastern Oregon.

"How to Comfort a Cold"
The poem "Invictus" is by William Ernest Henley.

"Out from Under"
In l890, Fay Fuller became the first Caucasian woman
to summit Mount Rainier.

"The Partial View"
This poem references "I Corinthians 13:12."

"Remembering 1950 Thanksgiving Days"
Lydia Marie Child wrote, *Over the meadow*...; E. Rutter
Leatham, the prayer, *Thank you, God* ...; and S. Baring-
Gould, *Now the day is over*... The idiom "madding crowd" is
from Thomas Gray.

"Return"
Martin Buber, an existentialist philosopher, wrote *I and
Thou*.

"Salt Loses Savor"
The phrase "surely goodness and mercy shall follow" is
from "Psalm 23."

"Tahoma"
This poem is after Yeats' "The Lake Isle of Innisfree."

"To Go to the Pond Because"
The epigraph combines phrases from "To Go to Lvov."

"Yesterday's Superstition"
The quilt-tossed cat refers to an old time quilting custom
and superstition. The unmarried place a cat in the middle
of a new quilt, folks grab the edges of the quilt, and flip it
up causing the cat to fly into the air. Whoever is closest to
the cat when it lands will be the next to marry.

Acknowledgments

Grateful acknowledgement is made to editors and staff of the following publications where these poems first appeared, some in earlier versions:

Abandoned Mine: "Refuge"

Caesura: "Past Seventy I Talk to Birds"

Cirque Literary Journal: "High Desert Wetlands"

The Closed Eye Open: "I'd Like to Lie Like the Sea Lies"

Clover, A Literary Rag: "Hike with Dead Cat" and "Out from Under"

The Comstock Review: "Freudian Pink Slip"

Creative Colloquy: "Beyond Nisqually" and "Tahoma"

Earth's Daughters: "Moonlit Walk"

The Lyric: "Deposed"

Passager: "Mystics Affirm Union with God is Blue Light"

Raven Chronicles: "Goodnight with Flights of Angels Singing"

Shark Reef, A Literary Magazine: "Misfit"

The Talking River Review: "Canticle for Auntie Ethel"

Unstamtic, A Micro Lit Mag: "To-do List"

Gratitude

My deep thanks to members of my writing groups, my numerous poetry teachers and workshop leaders, and to Olympia Poetry Network, the Richard Hugo House, the Port Townsend Writers Conference, the Colrain Poetry Conference, and LitFuse for providing rich learning opportunities.

Throughout the years that the poems of this collection percolated, specific individuals (among many) gave appreciated guidance on my poetry reading/writing and the manuscript process journey. They include April Ossmann, Joanne M. Clarkson, Deborah Woodard, Sarah Zale, Sarah Vap, and Kelli Russell Agodon.

A tremendous *thank you* goes to my editor and publisher Lana Hechtman Ayers of MoonPath Press, to designer Tonya Namura, and to the staff for their gracious generosity in giving of their time, wise helpfulness, and work to make this book a reality.

About the Author

From her beginning, Carol R. Sunde loved words and poetry. She delighted in her mother's dramatic renditions of nursery rhymes and poems such as "Up the Airy Mountain." Raised in Forest City, a small Iowa town, Carol attended St. Olaf College. After graduating with a degree in English and Speech Education, she toured the US for over a year with the Bishop's Company, a drama-in-the-church repertory organization. After her marriage to a fellow actor ended, Carol found employment as a social worker in Los Angeles, eventually earning a Masters and a Doctorate in Social Work. When she retired from a Grays Harbor College counselor position, she plunged into a lifelong interest in poetry by completing a Certificate in Poetry from the University of Washington.

Her poems have appeared in *Third Wednesday, The Comstock Review, Passager, Raven Chronicles, Shark Reef,* and elsewhere. One of her poems placed third in the 2023 Lakewold Garden Poetry Contest. Besides poetry, other top joys for Carol include yoga, bird and sky watching, travel, and camping on Mt. Rainier.

Carol lives a seven minute walk from the ocean in Westport, Washington. She feels lucky and privileged to be in the Pacific Northwest with its awesome people, forests, mountains, rivers, ocean, plains, volcanos, deserts, and, yes, rain.

www.ingramcontent.com/pod-product-compliance
Lightning Source LLC
Chambersburg PA
CBHW022103020426
42335CB00012B/808